"Journey of The Heart" Series

Vol. 2

"Brave Heart"

Clem Stack Publications Ltd.

POEMS

Poems are groups, of words,
brought to life,
by thoughts,
pen,
and ink.
Like the dew
of a thought,
the ink produces,
its magic
of combined words,
that can make,
you,
perhaps millions,
think.

Clement Stack
28/11/2004

CSP

Clem Stack Publications Ltd.

15, Flower Hill,
Rushbrooke Manor,
Cobh,
Co. Cork,
Ireland.

Tel. No. 021- 4812051
Email: clemstack@eircom.net

A copy of this book can be obtained from:

Trinity College, Dublin
The Universities of Oxford and Cambridge
The National Library of Scotland
The National Library of Wales

All rights reserved, please, no part of this publication may be reproduced, stored in a retrieval system, or transmitted in any form or by any means, electronic, mechanical, photocopying, recording, or otherwise, without the prior written permission of the publisher.
Permission is not nessecery for private use.

These poems are dedicated to the "brave heart"

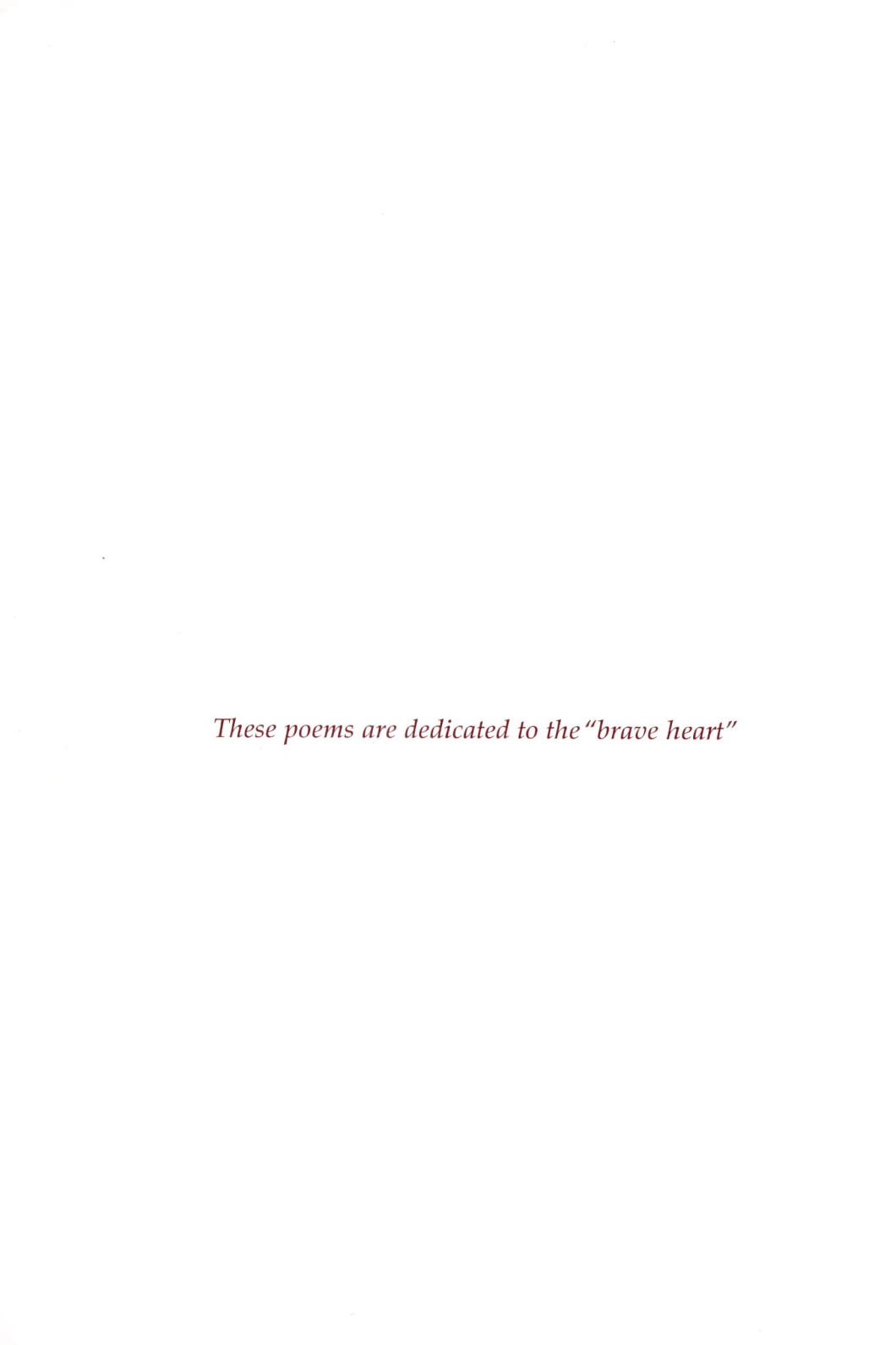

INDEX

1) BRAVE HEART 2
2) THE LONG NIGHT OF THE SOUL 4
3) LAUGHING IT OFF 5
4) A STEP AWAY 6
5) JUST FOR TODAY 7
6) FEELING DOWN 8
7) A SONG OF JOY 9
8) WHO IS EXPERIENCING WHO? 10
9) LA DARKNESS 11
10) ARE YOU THE ONE 12
11) TAKE A LITTLE DISTANCE 14
12) A THINKING GIFT 16
13) ALL LIES WITHIN 17
14) SPIRITUAL AWAKENESS 18
15) NOW SMILE 19
16) OR IS IT? 20

BRAVE HEART

Be brave heart,
be brave,
and lead me through the door
of the next stage of my life,
for this life is but a stage.
Be brave heart,
be brave, and lead me on
and I will follow.

Be brave heart,
be brave,
and lead me on to the next stage,
for I have wallowed in misery for too long.
Be brave heart,
be brave, and lead me on
for my army of confidence is being gathered.
Be brave heart,
be brave, and lead me on
and I will follow.

Be brave heart,
be brave,
for this is not an easy one,
the door to the next stage needs only to be opened.
Be brave heart,
be brave, and lead me on.
Be brave heart,
be brave,
for the dawn of new horizons,
are rising up from the chambers of courage.

Be brave heart,
be brave,
and lead me on,
for my army of confidence is arriving.
Be brave heart,
be brave, lead me forward,
and I will follow.

Let not the negative part of mind,
pull me down.
Be brave heart,
Be brave,
lead me on,
and I will follow.

Be brave heart,
Be brave,
Rise up, like the sun, to the freshness of tomorrows,
Be brave heart,
Be brave,
To say farewell to the setting of my sorrows.
Be brave heart,
Be brave,
lead me on,
and I will follow.

THE LONG NIGHT OF THE SOUL

Sun high,
spirit low.
Jammed in the traffic,
of going with the flow.
A cycle of reason,
to get up and go,
"Touché" to automatic pilot.

You're damned if you do,
damned if you don't,
damned if you can,
damned if you won't.
Damned is the well, of letting go.
So whose hands, are on the valves of reason.

Stuck in the here,
stuck in the now.
Fenced in emotions,
viewing their clarity.
Sun high,
spirits low,
whose crap, are you following anyway?

So you reach for your parachute,
in the season of desperation,
so well prepared, but lacking preparation.
As you jump into the void,
of your freedom within,
to pull the plug, on yourself

LAUGHING IT OFF

To laugh in defiance,
at circumstances prevailing,
as the heart is tested again.
Reviewing the situation,
without litigation,
to see the strength rise up from within.

To fall victim to the circumstance,
is two left feet,
doing the cosmic dance,
there is movement,
but awkward at its best.
So we smile in defiance,
at the circumstances prevailing,
which is half way to passing the test.

Tomorrow will bring another day,
to review the problems, in a different way,
Isn't that what tomorrows are all about.
So we conserve our energy force,
to get our ship back on course,
as we smile in defiance,
at the circumstances prevailing,
which is half way, to passing the test.

A STEP AWAY

Whatever you think is too high,
may not be too high at all.
Perhaps the focus of your attention,
was commandeered, by the fall.

And you never left the sun,
go down on your anger,
but the sun went down on you heart,
be brave to view your dawn,
when you are ready, make the start.

Stop crying for your freedom, in your night,
stop crying for your freedom, when you are full of fright,
search for your freedom, and discover your way,
for your freedom, is only a step away.

Don't be fearful, of your own dare,
just be vigilant, of your self set snare.
Try not to carry, more than your load,
as once was the prince, so once was the toad.

Your journey begins with the first step,
healing and love, are the fuel for the trip.
No hurry with pace, in rags or lace,
slow it down, and in your own pace.

Stop crying for your freedom, in your night,
stop crying for your freedom, when you are full of fright,
search for your freedom, and discover your way,
for your freedom, is only a step away.

JUST FOR TODAY

Just for today, take your heart out for a walk.
Just for today, count all the colours, that your eyes have seen.
Just for today, give thanks to your eyes.
Just for today, give thanks to your health.
Just for today, give thanks to your ears.
Just for today, give thanks to your organs.
Just for today, give thanks to your travelling suit.
Just for today, be silent and observe life.
Just for today, give thanks to your higher self.
Just for today, experience all of your problems,
and try not to let them experience you.
Just for today, be the listener of all the sounds.
Just for today, do not be yourself,
for without trying, you will be someone better.
Just for today, be still and observe all that is to be observed.
Just for today, and because of today,
tomorrow will be better.

FEELING DOWN

You can chalk it down,
even argue, the toss
a gain, is a gain,
a loss, is a loss.
One persons ceiling,
is another's floor,
will you, waste your energy,
in evening, the score?

Emotionally naked,
shaking, with the cold,
mentally, tormented,
one has to be bold,
to review, the situation,
as hot, voyages to cold,
where is this door to heaven?

The horizon of fear,
Is dawning again,
Life is a circus,
when penned, in the pen,
all the distractions,
in the heat wave of ice,
what is the currency, of circumstances?

A SONG OF JOY

Sometimes we sit in the fields of sorrow,
looking at the meadows,
displaying her colours of pain,
as we search,
with all our questions,
and things always, stay the same.

As we force a smile,
onto our faces,
our tears are going with the flow,
the sorrow fields are our answer,
because in here we can let it go.

For as we reach a point of understanding,
that this winter will turn to spring,
to hear once more the sound of laughter,
listen, the bells are about to ring.

So try not to stay there forever,
when you are ready,
open the gate, and come out,
and with all the silence,
that you can muster,
fill the air with your shout.

Sing your song of freedom,
sing your song of joy,
replace your tears with laughter,
and let your heart, come out to play,
on the spring, of this new day.

Yes, you will conquer your sorrow,
but memory will have her say,
your smile is your flag of freedom,
so sing your song of freedom,
sing your song of joy,
let all the unanswered questions,
go out with the tide.

WHO IS EXPERIENCING WHO?

O.K., so you have the right to feel angry,
but are you, experiencing your anger?
or is your anger, experiencing you?

O.K., so you have the right to feel sad,
but are you, experiencing your sadness?
or is your sadness, experiencing you?

O.K., so you have the right to feel bitter,
but are you, experiencing your bitterness?
or is your bitterness, experiencing you?

O.K., so you have the right to feel frustrated,
but are you, experiencing your frustration?
or is your frustration, experiencing you?

O.K., so you have the right to feel depressed,
but are you, experiencing your depression?
or is your depression, experiencing you?

O.K., so you have the right to your experience,
but are you, experiencing your experience?
or is your experience, experiencing you?

LA DARKNESS

If there was, no darkness in your life,
how would you recognise the light?
For darkness is very beautiful.
Greet the darkness,
in her many forms and shapes,
and she will guide you.

For the darkness, is where,
beautiful things can be found.

Are diamonds and gold,
not to be found in mother earth?

The beautiful naked body,
covered by the darkness of clothes.

The moon, the stars, all to be seen,
in the darkness of the night.

The darkness, of loneliness and aloneness,
to be dispelled, by the sight of a potential lover.

The darkness, of the womb,
to be dispelled, by the first
glorious appearance, into earthlight.

The darkness of your gloom,
may now generate room,
for you to wear a smile.

Close, softly now your eyes,
Inhale, softly, but deeply,
the fathoms of your darkness,
greet them, and thank your darkness.

For she is only guiding you,
To her friend the light.

Exhale your darkness,
after identifying her cause,
for you have,
experienced her effect.

ARE YOU THE ONE?

Are you the one,
who is travelling, your own distance?
Are you the one,
with your hands, on your own wheel,
Are you the one,
who has covered, all the angels?
If you are not the one, who is?

Are you the one,
who is blinded by your own blinkers?
Are you the one,
a troubled rock in your own stream?
Are you the one,
who listens to your own answers?
If you are not the one, who is?

Are you the one,
who bypasses all the signals?
Are you the one,
who stops when you should go?
Are you the one,
who never listens to your silence?
If you are not the one, who is?

Are you the one,
who is troubled by your situation?
Are you the one,
who seeks, to calm your stormy mind?
Are you the one,
who ignores your own answers?
If you are not the one, who is?

Are you the one,
who got soaked in the rains of torment?
Are you the one,
who dared not, to look within?

Are you the one,
whose sell date has expired?
If you are not the one, who is?
Will you be the one,
to cast away your own blinkers?
Will you be the one,
to take a grip on your own wheel?

Will you be the one,
to seek refuge in your own silence?
If you are not the one, who is?
If you are not the one, who is?

TAKE A LITTLE DISTANCE

Hang in,
hang tight,
but don't hang yourself.
Batten the spiritual hatches,
for this hurricane,
that is storming, the mind,
will pass.

They always do,
for nothing is permanent.
No storm, lasts forever,
the trick is to observe it,
to allow it, its freedom,
with no participation,
in its formatting.
No energising the situation,
for it has energy enough.

Try to watch it,
be the observer of the situation,
by not energising it,
with more thoughts.
Try not to play its games,
with all its devices, and spices,
it will pass,
it's guaranteed,
it always is.

The nets of the mind games,
will not snare you,
into non-reality.
The seeds of paranoia,
will bear no fruit.
The trick is to become the observer,
not the hired actor.

After practicing enough,
you will become,
the master of your own mind,
and it will work for you,
and not vice-versa.

Be in charge of the situation,
to the best of your ability,
and try not to let the situation,
be in charge of you.
If it was easy to do,
it would not be worth the effort.

A THINKING GIFT

The loneliness of being alone,
to stop, the heart from turning to stone,
the loneliness of being alone,
is a spark, for your fire.

As you seek to find uncontaminated love,
as graceful as the flight of the dove,
so why did God invent love?
and to whom must we surrender?

Of all the games that people play,
on this, or on, other days,
the de-icing of your heart,
is maybe, all that matters.

As the ice begins, to gently drip,
the cold feeling, will lose its grip,
you will shake loose from your ashes,
as your Phoenix flies out of your fire.

Your loneliness will disappear for good,
when the above is better understood,
understanding loneliness and aloneness,
will bring the gift of comfort.

ALL LIES WITHIN

Learn to be patient with yourself,
to trust yourself,
to take the time to find yourself,
to get to know your higher self.

All will be revealed in good time.

Take the time to be patient with yourself,
take the time to trust yourself,
take the time to find yourself,
take the time to grow into your higher self.

Time is a cosmic currency,
so spend your currency of "time" well.

And as you learn to be patient with your-
self,
and as you learn to trust yourself,
you will surely, get to find yourself,
and in time you will become your higher
self.

For all lies within.

P.S. If you practice enough patience,
    you will never become the patient.

SPIRITUAL AWAKENESS

For deep was your night,
and deep was your fright,
and deep is your love and laughter.
And deep were your ways,
and deep were your stays,
and deep was your night to remember.

And deep was your thought,
at the sorrow, ego brought,
and deep was your garden of remembrance.
And deep flowed your tears,
and deep were the fears,
as you struggled to find life's meaning.

And deeper than deep,
your eyes did weep,
at the loss of something enchanted.
And deeper than deep,
your eyes did weep,
as nature proceeded with her canting.

And deep were your fears,
and deep were your tears,
and deep was your garden of remembrance.
And deep was your night,
and deep was your fright,
all turning to bubbles of laughter.

NOW SMILE

Be ready and receptive,
for whatever the moment might offer.
Be more open to your unknown,
and invite her in.

Cultivate the invisible, or the unknown,
and in good time,
the invisible will become visible,
the unknown, the known.

Take time to witness,
the activities of the mind,
and she will show you how,
to cultivate your now.

The now is no more than this instant,
this precious present moment,
for to live in her presence,
is to live in awareness,
the awareness of your now.

When you learn to accept your now,
regardless of what she has to offer,
your mind will become calmer,
and you will wear, your smile permanently.

OR IS IT?

And if there is nothing more to believe in,
and you do not give a toss,
perhaps it is time to journey inwards,
and evaluate this so called loss.

And if, there is nothing more to believe in,
and so-called friends, hold no more sway,
evaluating, the situation,
is the spiritual order of the day.

And if there is nothing more to believe in,
and happiness is just a nine letter word,
cross roads, lead to confusion,
a new direction seems so absurd.

Or is it?

The Spiritual Fields

Clem Stack

"Follow the trail series"

This impressive book sparkles with wit, insight and uplift and one cannot fail to be enriched by this author's positive and engaging approach to life. There is a judicious balancing of practice and precept in the structuring of the text, and lively scenarios are offered as affirmations of the concepts which the author has chosen to expound.

The text is totally free from any of the tiresome pretensions one has come to associate with literature of this sort, and Clem Stack has made it his business to demystify the workings of the mind and spirit and to demonstrate that untold degrees of enlightenment, i.e. the raising of our spiritual consciousness, are within our reach if we take the time to formulate a positive way of thinking. The author's great good humour shines forth from the text to the extent that we never feel as though he is condescending or preaching from a great and superior height.

This is a friendly book, and its author has much to share. The engaging style and thoughtful presentation will ensure that this book will be of appeal to a broad cross section of readers.

Future book titles:

The Spiritual Letters
The Spiritual Warrior

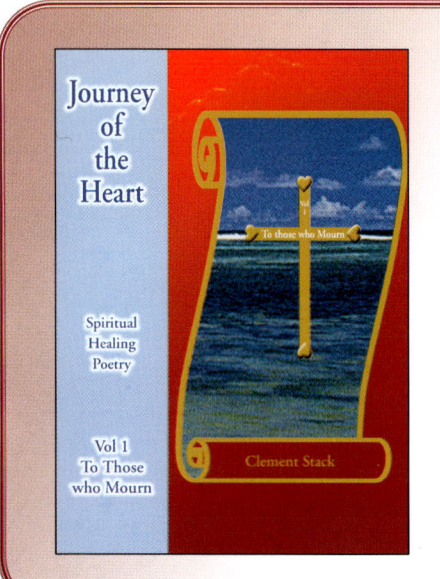

These poems, are dedicated, to those who are experiencing, the experience of mourning. They were written, to bring comfort, and understanding, to you and your loved ones. In our age of human evolution, death is still surrounded in mysterious veils. These veils are fast, disintegrating, as we enter a new age, of understanding. Remember, we are spiritual beings, having a human experience, not human beings enjoying a spiritual experience. We come from there (home) so we must return to there.

Journey of the Heart Series

Vol. 2   Be brave heart

Vol. 3   Voyage of the heart

Vol. 4 -10 (to follow)